REPTILES

KOMODO DRAGONS

BY MELISSA ROSS

WWW.APEXEDITIONS.COM

Copyright © 2024 by Apex Editions, Mendota Heights, MN 55120. All rights reserved. No part of this book may be reproduced or utilized in any form or by any means without written permission from the publisher.

Apex is distributed by North Star Editions:
sales@northstareditions.com | 888-417-0195

Produced for Apex by Red Line Editorial.

Photographs ©: Shutterstock Images, cover, 4–5, 6–7, 9, 16–17, 18–19, 20, 22–23, 24, 25, 26–27; iStockphoto, 1, 8, 10–11, 12–13, 14–15, 21, 29

Library of Congress Control Number: 2022920183

ISBN
978-1-63738-548-7 (hardcover)
978-1-63738-602-6 (paperback)
978-1-63738-707-8 (ebook pdf)
978-1-63738-656-9 (hosted ebook)

Printed in the United States of America
Mankato, MN
082023

NOTE TO PARENTS AND EDUCATORS

Apex books are designed to build literacy skills in striving readers. Exciting, high-interest content attracts and holds readers' attention. The text is carefully leveled to allow students to achieve success quickly. Additional features, such as bolded glossary words for difficult terms, help build comprehension.

CHAPTER 1
A SUDDEN ATTACK 4

CHAPTER 2
LARGE LIZARDS 10

CHAPTER 3
FINDING FOOD 16

CHAPTER 4
LIFE CYCLE 22

COMPREHENSION QUESTIONS • 28
GLOSSARY • 30
TO LEARN MORE • 31
ABOUT THE AUTHOR • 31
INDEX • 32

CHAPTER 1

A SUDDEN ATTACK

A Komodo dragon hides in the grass. It stays still and waits. Finally, it spots a deer walking by.

Komodo dragons can stay in the same spot for hours when they are hunting.

The giant lizard lunges. It bites down on the deer's leg. Its sharp claws grab tight. But the deer wriggles free. It runs away.

Komodo dragons usually hunt in the daytime.

FAST FACT
Komodo dragons are fast. They can run up to 13 miles per hour (21 km/h).

Komodo dragons often wait until animals die. Then they eat them.

But the hunt isn't over. The Komodo dragon follows the bleeding deer's scent. It finds the deer and eats it.

SENSE OF SMELL

Komodo dragons use their tongues to smell. They flick their tongues in and out of their mouths. They pick up scents in the air. Then they follow the scents to find food.

Komodo dragons can smell animals up to 1 mile (1.6 km) away.

CHAPTER 2

LARGE LIZARDS

Komodo dragons are giant **reptiles**. They can grow more than 10 feet (3 m) long. And they can weigh more than 300 pounds (136 kg).

Komodo dragons are the biggest lizards on Earth.

Komodo dragons live on five islands in Indonesia. These places are warm and wet. Their hills, forests, and grasslands provide **habitats** for Komodo dragons.

FAST FACT

Komodo dragons are excellent swimmers.

Most Komodo dragons live on Komodo Island.

A Komodo dragon's tail is almost as long as its body.

14

Komodo dragons have thick skin and long claws. They also have powerful tails. They sometimes swing their strong tails to hit **prey**.

DIG AND REST

Komodo dragons use their sharp claws to dig holes. On hot days, the lizards stay in the holes to keep cool. The holes also help Komodo dragons stay warm at night.

CHAPTER 3

Finding Food

Komodo dragons are **carnivores**. They eat large and small animals. Most Komodo dragons hunt alone. But sometimes they share the same kill.

16

Komodo dragons often eat rodents, deer, and goats.

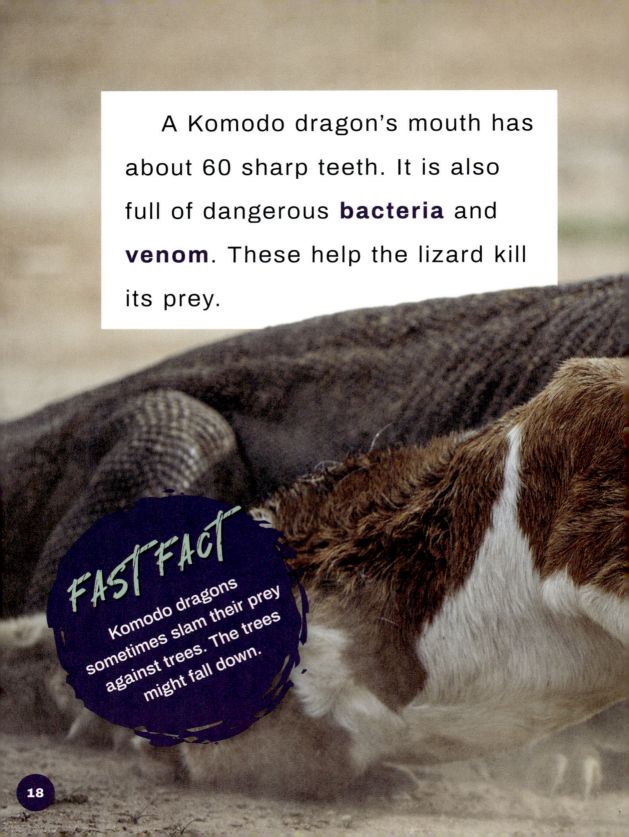

A Komodo dragon's mouth has about 60 sharp teeth. It is also full of dangerous **bacteria** and **venom**. These help the lizard kill its prey.

FAST FACT
Komodo dragons sometimes slam their prey against trees. The trees might fall down.

Komodo dragons usually eat their prey whole. They even eat skin, bones, and hooves.

Adult Komodo dragons are fast and strong.

Adult Komodo dragons don't have **predators**. But baby Komodo dragons do. Adult Komodo dragons often eat them.

FACING DANGER

People sometimes hunt Komodo dragons. As a result, the lizards have become **endangered**. To help, people pass laws against hunting. They also create protected areas where the lizards can live.

Komodo Island is part of Komodo National Park. The park was made to protect Komodo dragons.

CHAPTER 4

LIFE CYCLE

Komodo dragons usually live alone. But they may come together to **mate** in summer. Sometimes males fight one another. The winner can mate with a female.

Komodo dragons sometimes fight over territory.

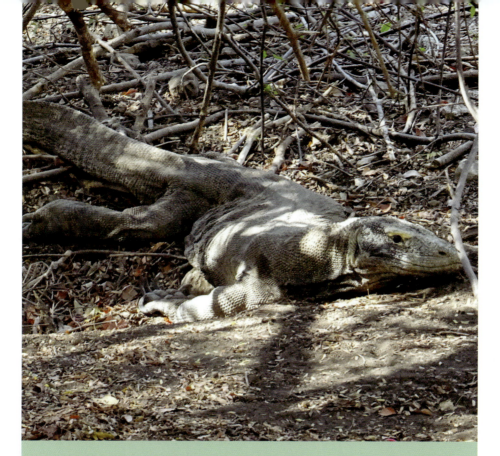

Female Komodo dragons dig nests in the ground to lay their eggs.

After mating, females lay up to 30 eggs. Then, the females guard the eggs for a few months until the eggs hatch.

MALES NOT NEEDED

Some female Komodo dragons can have babies without mating. They lay eggs on their own. When this happens, only male babies hatch from the eggs.

Newly hatched Komodo dragons are about 13 inches (33 cm) long.

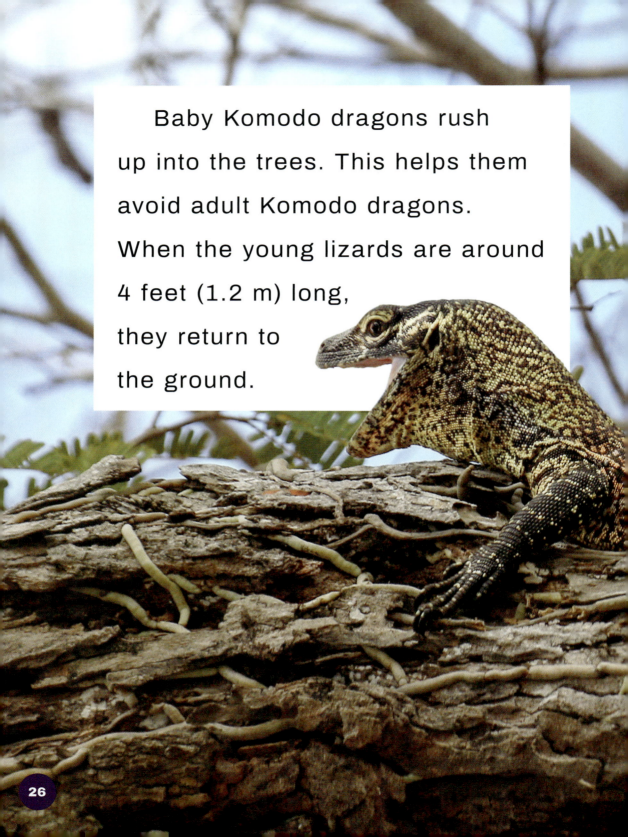

Baby Komodo dragons rush up into the trees. This helps them avoid adult Komodo dragons. When the young lizards are around 4 feet (1.2 m) long, they return to the ground.

FAST FACT

Komodo dragons normally live about 30 years in the wild.

Young Komodo dragons stay in the trees for about four years.

COMPREHENSION QUESTIONS

Write your answers on a separate piece of paper.

1. Write a few sentences describing how Komodo dragons hunt their prey.

2. What fact about Komodo dragons is the most interesting to you? Why?

3. How long can Komodo dragons grow?
    - A. less than 4 feet
    - B. more than 10 feet
    - C. about 60 feet

4. Why do baby Komodo dragons need to stay away from adults?
    - A. Adult Komodo dragons give them food.
    - B. Adult Komodo dragons take their food.
    - C. Adult Komodo dragons might eat them.

5. What does **lunges** mean in this book?

*The giant lizard **lunges**. It bites down on the deer's leg.*

- **A.** shakes back and forth
- **B.** jumps and attacks
- **C.** spins around

6. What does **flick** mean in this book?

*Komodo dragons use their tongues to smell. They **flick** their tongues in and out of their mouths.*

- **A.** hit something hard
- **B.** hold still
- **C.** move quickly

Answer key on page 32.

GLOSSARY

bacteria
Tiny living things that can make people or animals sick.

carnivores
Animals that eat meat.

endangered
In danger of dying out forever.

habitats
The places where animals normally live.

mate
To form a pair and come together to have babies.

predators
Animals that hunt and eat other animals.

prey
Animals that are hunted and eaten by other animals.

reptiles
Cold-blooded animals that have scales.

venom
A poison made by an animal and used to bite or sting prey.

BOOKS

Ringstad, Arnold. *Totally Amazing Facts about Reptiles*. North Mankato, MN: Capstone Press, 2018.

Sommer, Nathan. *Komodo Dragon vs. Orangutan*. Minneapolis: Bellwether Media, 2021.

Spalding, Maddie. *Komodo Dragons*. North Mankato, MN: Capstone Press, 2020.

ONLINE RESOURCES

Visit **www.apexeditions.com** to find links and resources related to this title.

ABOUT THE AUTHOR

Melissa Ross is the author of *Forensics for Kids* and other educational books for children. When she's not busy researching and writing, she enjoys spending time with family, drawing, painting, and hiking.

INDEX

B
bacteria, 18

C
carnivores, 16

E
eggs, 24–25
endangered, 21

H
habitats, 12

I
Indonesia, 12

M
mating, 22, 24–25

P
predators, 20
prey, 15, 18

R
reptiles, 10

S
smell, 8–9
swim, 13

T
tongues, 9

V
venom, 18

ANSWER KEY:
1. Answers will vary; 2. Answers will vary; 3. B; 4. C; 5. B; 6. C